RESCUING OUR HUMAN

VISITATIONS FROM ABOVE and BEYOND

LOUISE Y. FURMAN

FOREWORD

What is man

without the beasts?

If all the beasts

were gone

man would die

from a great

loneliness

of the

Spirit

CHIEF SEATTLE

RESCUING OUR HUMAN

VISITATIONS FROM ABOVE and BEYOND

Copyright © 2024 **LYF Publishing**

All rights reserved. No part of this publication may be reproduced, distributed, or transmitted in any form or by any means, including photocopying, recording, or other electronic or mechanical methods, without the prior written permission of the publisher, except in the case of brief quotations embodied in critical reviews and certain other noncommercial uses permitted by copyright law. For permission requests, write to the publisher, addressed "Attention: Book Rights and Permission," at the address below.

Published in the United States of America

ISBN 978-1-963379-07-5 (SC)

LYF Publishing
222 West 6th Street
Suite 400, San Pedro, CA, 90731
www.stellarliterary.com

Order Information and Rights Permission:

Quantity sales. Special discounts might be available on quantity purchases by corporations, associations, and others. For details, contact the publisher at the address above.

For Book Rights Adaptation and other Rights Permission.
Call us at toll-free 1-888-945-8513 or send us an email at admin@stellarliterary.com.

INTRODUCTION

It has long been a point of fact that we humans do not rescue the animals around us, but rather that it is we who are usually the rescued; rescued from our loneliness, our self-absorption, our incessant quest for the unattainable, or our basic lack of survival instinct.

The following insights delve into what effect eleven canines, felines and equines have had on a spanse of one human's life. How, indeed, their very presence, day by day, hour by hour, and year by year, have contributed not only to the well-being, but to the virtual survival of a certain human.

Often it is only in looking back can the import of these creature lives be realized. a truth that each of your readers will soon realize.

This first visitation is initiated by Chloe, the spirit Cat who returns in a soft cloud to check on her human. she appears to the current caretaker, canine Quincy, who is looking just a bit lonely these days. Chloe's mission is to conjure up all of the previous creatures in the human's life to support this little Corgi mix pup.

Each canine, feline, equine, and yes, even the birds makes themselves known in ROLL CALL, an exercise in which Chloe is "boss lady"

In subsequent segments, these special departed creatures describe not only CLOSE CALLS that they had lived through, but major events in the human's life that required their rescue of her.

It is also not beyond them to chit-chat together, recounting lives that they had shared while in the household of their human, as evidenced by the occasional foto.

Finally, after identifying not only with the creatures, but with the common life events of humans, the reader is encouraged to comprise his/her own list of RESCUERS.

In doing so, we will be honoring all of those creatures who were there for us.

The final pages of this book are for you, the reader, to enter in those creatures which have been in your lives-lest you forget.

A VISIT FROM CAT CHLOE

Laying on the floor of the human's home in deep repose, is a beautiful mound of deep auburn, wavy fur. Belly to the sky, paws dropped to chest, tail fanned out, tongue drooping out of his jaw, the pup's only sign of life is the occasional yelp generated by a deep dream. Indeed, Quincy is "dead--to-the-world ", quite unaware of an imminent encounter with the spirit of a special feline friend.
    Chloe gently coaxes Quincy into wakefulness.

    Stretching into his full body length of four feet, Quincy's short Corgi-Like legs reach to the ceiling passing directly through the hovering apparition. Finally fully emerged, Quincy says (in creature talk, of course)
    '"Chloe? Is that you? ...but where is the rest of you?"
    "Oh, you mean my guts, and lungs and stuff I needed for my earth life?"
    "Well-yeah"
    "I shed all that heavy stuff the day I took that step beyond
    "Yeah-I remember that day Chloz. Not good of you to leave me like that. Now I'm stuck with taking care of the human by myself!
    "Well dear, my clock ran out after 12 years as will yours someday too
(I can only hope. ...)

    "So, Chloz, what are you doing here? Appearing out of nowhere like this?
    "I came to check on you and the human. To be sure that everything's pushing along o.k."
    "Nice of you to remember us incidental earthlings. But why now?"
    "I spent 10 years of my earth life with that human and I want to be sure she's on the right track"
    "And you do that—--how?" Quincy is still yawning himself awake.

"With the help of all of us who were in her life all along. All of us who were saving her when she never realized it. The whole crew has come along with me. We spent so much of our earth lives in her life that, well, she's our responsibility!

With this promise of Spirit back-up, Quincy stretched himself into a new, confident posture, ready to take on whatever his human brought his way!

Quincy actual pose

ROLL CALL

The Chloe Spirit now elevated herself on staunch legs, raised her back, and called out to a small cadre of creature spirits hitherto seen and heard only by Quincy.

"OK Guys!!" yelled Chloe "Listen up!!" she yelled. (in as much as a soft and gentle feline was able to yell)

"Let's remember why we're here, ok? We've come to pump up this little Quincy fella and share what we know about our Human so he can do his job better. So what I want you to do is to line up, state your species, and tell him what part of Human's life you each were present for.

Got that?

All creatures great and small nodded their consent in humble creature agreement.

"You're first up Mink"

MINK:

I'm a Heinz 57 variety pup that lived with our young human in her early years on the Jersey Shore. It was just her and me most of the time since her Mom was always away working. I saw her through the death if her beloved Aunt Belle who rescued the little tyke when the Mom got really really ill and went away for a long time. After the Mom got better, my young human still saw Aunt Belle as her Mom. So when it was time for Auntie to cross over, my 13 year old human was shattered. She sobbed into my furry neck day after day after day. All I could do was to be there, warm and comforting.

Tinker Bell

I'm a lovely cheery, pretty little blue parakeet that lived at Aunt Belle's for many years. Our little human came to visit every summer and was sure she could teach me to talk, but I never let her. One day they forgot and left my cage door open, and after a few flights around the house I made it to the outside world. Freedom!!!!

SPORT

"I'm a beautiful little beagle that joined the family (that is...only the Mom and the kid) in Long Island City, NY.

It was over the time of the killing of the American President, Kennedy. The human girl was in nursing school, across the river in Jersey. Her Mom and I lived in a little basement apartment in Queens where I always gave the gal a super welcome when she came home. One day the neighbor came to say there was a call for my family–not having a phone ourselves–and when the Mom walked in the door I could tell it was NOT a good call. My human's brother is dead.

The Marines will bring his body home by train.

*******SNOOPY of California

I, too, am an adorable Beagle. (Our human seems to have a weakness for our breed)

She got me as a gift back there in Baltimore, Md. Little did I know that I would be flown clear out to an Air Force Base in California. And little did I know that, even as a lowly Second Lieutenant., my human was picked (aka ordered) to go out to IKE'S house to take care of him for the flu. She and this neat man (aka General, former President) became good friends and kept in touch. She told me all about it when she would come home, so tired---but happy.

PRINCESS

I am one of California Snoopy's kids. Mom and our human kept me after my brothers and sisters went to new homes. (Probably because I looked the most like Mom.) I was one spoiled puppy!

"She's my kid !!"

NOCHE

"I am an adorable, black, curly-haired and very smart Cock-a-poo that my human found on a snowy night in Salem Oregon. She called me Nieve Noche (Snowy Night) having just gotten back from 3.5 months on a floating campus, the last stops being countries in South America.

I was so little when she chose me that she tucked me into her coat to bring me to her place!

Little did I know how many milestones in her life that I would be there for over the next 12 years! I was there for her when no one else was: a surprise baby, long hospital shifts, a rocky marriage, a boat load of kids that didn't appreciate me, another baby and finally an escape to find our own lives. Don't ask me to count the moves !"

SO SO

"I'm the most beautiful, large, long haired gray feline that you will ever meet. I met my human in Salem, OR . and, along with Noche, traveled through some of her toughest spots with her.

I saw other kitties come and go, and was always grateful for their company, but I was always top cat in those years. Like my buddy Noche, I also had a long shelf life. Twelve earth years is quite a lot, especially with all those changes going on. I especially loved being cuddled by my human's first born girl. We had a special understanding"

BABE

"I'm an Appaloosa Mare born under the name of Little Moon. My human found me at Silver Creek Falls Christian Retreat center. Her family would donate gallons of milk which she herself had milked from Boss the cow. I understood later that that was her way of pulling away from the chaos of seven kids.

Before my owner would let me go, my human had to come up to the center a few times a week to be sure she knew how to ride and care for me. I was patient with her clumsiness, but as time went on I made a proper horse person out of her as we galloped around the arena. I was having a swell time there in Central Oregon, a fourteen year old on my back as we chased small herds of deer and jumped across irrigation ditches. I spent 15 years with her smaller family of three.

From my nice large pasture I could see my strong human hefting my hay bales out of her Honda, pounding the thick ice in the pond so I could drink, and of course splitting wood.. Those were rough winters all right, but I had SoSo, Noche, Snoopy and Muffin with me. Quite the family."

SNOOPY- of Oregon

"I'm a handsome black n' white pitbull and hound mix. I was a birthday gift to the second born for her 7th year. The cutest little pup was I !! Little did I know that I would spend the next 12 years with my family and clock so many, many miles of travel with them. Oregon to California time and time again and even all over New Mexico. Would my life in the back seat ever end ??!!

I became my human's main pup as her girls grew up and went off to college. I was never to be lonely with all of the cats that came in and out of our lives".

MUFFIN

"I'm a tri -colored Border Collie mix. I came to live with the family when the landlord of the place they rented decided that he would give me to them. I fit in really good with Noche, Snoopy, Babe and all matter of cats coming and going. It was short-lived when a neighbor hit me with his car and I came to Above and Beyond way too early.

BUDDY

"I'm a handsome tri-colored Foxhound that got from Missouri to Payson, AZ. My human and me met up there in the White Mountains and we began our Arizona life together. Our best move was to Flagstaff where I loved the mountains and free outdoorsy life. One day she came home from a nursing gig with two little puppies that she rescued from the Peach Springs Reservation;, so there I was, puppy sitter in chief. I made one cross country trip with her (which I'll tell you about later)

We lived in very special places like Flagstaff, Carson City, Tahoe and Topaz Lake. Perfect country for a pup like me.

Buddy has lived in some great places

Tahoe Flagstaff, Carson City,
Topaz Lake

HELP FOR QUINCY

The cloud of Spirits gathered round Quincy, exuding a great sense of comfort and camaraderie. They listened to the challenges he was presently facing and bolstered his ego as best they could.

Their human carried on with her daily living, unaware of the increased population in the house in keeping with the occasional lack of awareness of humans. Little did she know that her well being was now being discussed by a host of very illusive, intelligent, and sensitive spirit creatures.

"Hey Quince! I think I know just what you need- a buddy to help you with your human care!""

"Yeah Chloe. That's just what he needs. How do we go about doing that anyway? "asks Noche.

"Well, there's a place in town called Mutt Matchers that might help us out. I floated past there yesterday and saw a new pup that just arrived from New Mexico. She was pretty tuckered from the trip, poor thing. I'll put a bug in our human's ear to go on down there and find her."

And so she did.

That night their human had a dream about Quincy romping around with a neat little black and white pup.

Within a few days the match had been made. Quincy now had his new sister who proved to be great company. Truth be told, in her happiness to be free of shelter life, Dakota really had no idea of the responsibility awaiting her.

"Time enough for that later. They just need to have fun for now" said Chloe.

Despite the difference in their age and personality, the pups got on well.

Dakota soon learned that, despite his gentle looks, Quincy was still Alpha Dog.

She deferred to him at mealtime, and through mere body language and subtle mental images, Quincy showed her the rules of the residence. Submissive and sweet, Dakota was eager to please.

"NO! NO! N-O-O!" yells Quincy. "You can NOT pee on the living room carpet!"

Yeah, Dakota, Chloe and I were great buddies

Dakota freezes in her pee-crouch whining "But, but nobody was around to let me out…."

"She's right" Chimes in Spirit Chloe. "It's not like that for us felines who have that kitty box to go to. Looks like you have a lot more teaching to do, buddy"

Their human dutifully scrubs out the mistake and reaches for the deodorizer.

Then in a fond embrace of the thick, soft fur of her newest creature. Dakota's tongue casts loving kisses all over her human's face.
    Forgiveness should be soft and warm.

"So, Quince, tell me about her", Dakota wants to know about her new human.

"Where to start. Chloe was still here when I came. For a cat she was a real Boss Lady. Really kept me in my place."

In fact, our human and Chloe spent the better part of a decade together. Moves came as frequently as TV commercials. The most memorable were their days in Mexico where life was cheap and close to the sea."

Chloe had full freedom of their Hispanic neighborhood, yet always came back to their door for her requisite meal.
Sacked up in her soft carrier, Chloe often went to the sandy reaches of the playa, taking in the new scents of sea birds and YES!! FISH!!.

The border crossings at Tijuana were a bear. Hours at a time of hawkers coming to lines of cars, dispensing leaflets of Salvation or offering to clean headlights. Once Stateside and in their "frugal" motel, cat and human re-learned daily American living. Even in their multi-unit motel, Chloe would return to the right room, scratching and meowing to be let in.
Their migration of many miles and many homes at last came to an end in Arizona where they would have a home of their own. Not a really "up market" place, it needed a lot of elbow grease. Best of all, it had tons of trees, birds and wildlife all around just to make it very interesting.
"Especially for a cat !" adds Chloe.

"So how did you come into the picture, Quince?"

"Our human somehow knew that Chloe was reaching the end of her earth years and would enjoy some creature company. So I came to live with them and perked Chloe' life up a bit.
We went everywhere with our human. We especially loved those time at the Big Water"

"Big Water?"

"The Pacific Ocean of course!"

The next two years were family bliss as the three adjusted to each other.
As always happens, one never knows when the last day of being together would come to an end.
It was on Good Friday when Chloe took her step to Above and Beyond.

"What did you do?" asked Dakota.

"We looked all over for her -couldn't find her anywhere; not even a sign that the coyotes got her. I figure she just went—UP!'

"That's exactly how it was" recalls Chloe." a soft, warm current took me home"

CLOSE CALLS AND TIGHT PLACES

   Manifesting themselves gently around Dakota not to frighten her, all of the creature spirits assembled to regale her with their stories of past lives with their human.
   Occasionally Quincy wanders into the conversation to describe present day events of tight spots for his human. Dakota, so new and naive to the challenges of human-care simply lays down, chin on paws. And listens in awe.

   "Well, we did have that RUN-AWAY DAY one spring morning in Oregon" recounts BABE.
   "My human decided it was a fine day to saddle me up and take her 5 year old out for a ride. So she heaved the little girl up onto my haunches and hefted herself into the saddle.
   Off we went, clippity clop, clippity clop in my usual musical rhythm. We were quite the happy trio until the heavens opened and poured hail onto my tender skin. I took off, as they say, like a bat out of hell, my poor human clenching her kid, digging her knees into my sides, and being not the least successful

in reigning me in. The winds picked up and the hail battered us even worse at my full speed ahead down the blacktop road. It's a wonder that my shoes didn't skip from under us!"

"Good grief Babe. What did you do?!" inquires wide-eyed Buddy.

"Well, my human led me onto the dirt berm and reigned me in as best she could, shaking as bad as she was. The storm finally let up and talking to me as gently as she could, she eased her little girl onto the ground. She set her over under a tree, then came to me and stroked my face thanking me for not throwing them"

"Then what?"

"Well, my human was afraid to ride the three of us that distance back to the house, so she waved down a passing car and asked them to take the little girl home so that she could follow on me."

"That was taking a bit of a chance, total strangers taking her kid" warned Buddy.

"Sure was, but my human has always been a trusting spirit and her kid was waiting for us when we got back, telling the siblings about how we almost got killed."

"It was a day to remember all right. My human learned to trust me, and I learned how to trust her."

The stories continued, revealing sometimes unimaginable events.

"Well, I had one of those near death events too!" chimes in feline Zoe.

Snoopy comforts Zoe after her very close call

My human would take me up into open fields after her shift so I could be free and sniff out new stuff, a trusting spirit as you say."

"This one night we got separated and she couldn't find me before the sun set. She had to go home without me, feeling really crummy. Needless to say it was one heck of a light for this little cat person. An owl came down and grabbed the top of my head to take me away, but I wriggled free and fell to the ground. Ouch! And my head bleeding at that!"

"How did you survive that long night Zoe? It sounds terrible!"

"It wasn't an easy time. I had to climb up a tree and hide til daybreak. My head hurt SO bad!!"

"How did you get back to our human?"

"Well…that's the miracle of it. She came looking for me after her night shift and found me pitifully crouching there on the ground not far from where we were last night. She bundled me up into her warm coat, kissed me on my injured head, and brought me home. I was one happy kitty"

"So you almost spent one of your lives on that one, huh?"

"Yeah. That hawk thought he could carry me off but I fought him off"

Not to be outdone in the crisis category, Quincy and Dakota have a few human close calls of their own to share.

"So, Quince and Dakota, we figger those scary times are past now that she is older, right?" The Spirits lean in expectantly.

Quincy and Dakota rise onto all fours and strike a distinguished pose as they prepare to take their turn on stage.

"Oh no, age hasn't managed to keep our human out of tight spots. Mostly it's her body that has taken a beating" offers Quincy.

Dakota provides details of the first incident.

"We were happily romping around the dog park in Flagstaff when one of our more robust canines plowed into our girl and threw her down, her lower leg pointing where it shouldn't be.

"People gathered round to help but it was a real O-U-C-H moment.

A nice lady got the two of us into the car while our human limped along, the real pain not catching up yet. At Mc D's she got a big bag of ice to keep on her gas pedal leg for the next 150 miles til home.".
"The best we could do for her was to be still and quiet"

"Yeah, because she thought it was just a sprain, she didn't get to the Doc for a week. Getting us fed was hard, and our runs were cut way down. She had to just watch from the car."

Dakota adds, "Then the Doc put this big old clumsy boot thingy on her leg and expected her to drive home with that thing on. There we were, waiting at home, wondering if we'd ever see her again. Scary."

"Yikes!" exclaims Sport. "How long did THAT go on?!"

"She was back to almost normal in two months but it was a tough go. No neighbors to help; friends were away. Just us, snuggling nearby and not being too demanding."

"We're really proud of you guys. Good work" says Chloe, smiling.

They debated telling the Spirits that it only got worse, like the time she was doing a good deed for this homeless fella and ended up getting seriously bitten by his dog.

They figured that story could wait for another time.

LITTLE FOLKS WITH BIG PROBLEMS

A substantial part of their human's nursing career was spent caring for children with major disabilities Whether from birth trauma, near drowning, or congenital defects, these children and their families were on a journey not to be envied.

Several of the nurses' dogs had gone along over the course of these assignments with permission of the parents, of course. Invariably the children responded to the presence of the loving animals and the families were quick to notice.

Buddy was a frequent visitor to 2 year old Janie who suffered from intractable seizures requiring the right frontal lobe of her brain to be removed. Later, it was necessary for the entire right hemisphere to go as well Yet, as only the young are able, Janie was versatile and compensated through the other parts of her brain. Through it all, both Buddy and his human tapped into parts of Janie's spirit that neither medication nor intricate procedure could touch.

Her Spirit.

"I sure liked that little tyke. We had great fun together. Once, the physical therapist left after a session pretty frustrated that Janie couldn't or wouldn't do a certain task. So after she was gone, I fetched the frisbee and shook it in front of my little buddy. She grabbed it, just a little wobbly and tossed it for me to retrieve! The games had begun!"

As Janie grew older she was able to enjoy the therapeutic wonder of Medicine Horse and later Compassionate Reins, programs that allowed disabled children to increase their physical abilities and coordination through the movement of their steeds.

"Yep. That's what we do all right" adds Babe. "Though I never met Janie herself, I heard a lot about her from my human. We horses do have a special bond with the human lot, but its especially stronger with the younguns because their spirits are still so young, and fresh, and fearless"

Another child who suffered a multitude of birth defects also enjoyed free afternoons after therapy with nurse's pup Buddy. Kylee's parents granted her nurse permission to take her around town, to the park and even to her apartment. There Buddy would welcome the company of the toddler. Buddy recalls " I was always happy to hear their footsteps at our door 'cause I was home alone while my human worked. The little girl would brighten up and laugh when she saw me; I guess she had a hard workout at therapy, so it was playtime !

FARMING US OUT

After hearing about her creatures' encounter with the Little Folk, Spirit Chloe shook her head in a sudden "deja vu" moment.

"Yes, I did something like that" as she struggled to remember.

"Yes, I know now-it was up in San Francisco at the house of my human's daughter.
She was keeping me while her Mom was in Africa; it turned out I did some of the "keeping" myself"

Our daughter became quite sickly at one point and later reported to her Mom that Chloe came in very close and wouldn't leave her until she was better.

"Yes, the gal was pretty miserable -no doubt the flu. I wasn't all that great myself after flying clear up there in the hold of a plane from Arizona. I'd never done that before and NEVER WILL again !!"

The other Spirits related in a heartbeat, agreeing that each and every time that their human set off for Kenya, they were destined to be farmed out for a month or two. It was always with good folks and often with really other people who had really fun creatures, yet each time they were never quite sure if they would see their human again.
After all, she was half way around the world, not sunbathing in Cabo.

Chloe says " I think I take the prize for the most "live-overs" but let's take a talley just for the fun of it"
All agreed, each spirit was convinced that they would be the winner.

California Snoopy: "Only once, but it was a LONG time! She was on that floating campus drifting all over the world for that full semester at sea. Many of us noticed she was a really different person when she came back. I guess you can't go to 21 countries and see all that without being changed"

Oregon Snoopy: "She was raising two kids alone and working when I had her., no time much less any money to travel anywhere except maybe to McDonald's on a free day.

Buddy: "I stayed with a family in Carson City while she was in Egypt and Kenya for 6 weeks. She left me only once, so I guess I'm not in the running"

Quincy: " Well folks , I guess I came in at the peak of her travel life . I've had six " live-overs" with kind people. Each one was pretty long because she started doing important work over there in Kenya. The Covid epidemic put the brakes on all that , so I'm glad she's stuck at home now"

Moderator Chloe Cat: "Well that does it. I only had four live-overs for those Africa treks so QUINCY IS THE WINNER!!!!

"What did I win Chloz?"

"You won the knowledge that you will probably never have to be left again!"

("Probably??)
"OK…I'll take it !!! " says Quincy.

Indeed as the human got older the home front was looking better and better. She could live without all those airport layovers, that jet lag, that culture shock, that conversion of currency, those WC's, and just unreliable living in general.
Hard work for an aging human.

BEANS AND RICE

Quincy and Dakota bring the Spirit Creatures up to date on their human's recent life, the forefront of which is her connection with the East African country of Kenya.

"Yep, those trips over there were the reason for my six farming -out gigs" says Quincy.
"But she always came back so happy, and filled with so many neat stories about life over there, alot of it pretty hard to believe!"

It was always a challenge to find who could be trusted with her precious pup for the 2-3 months that she would be gone. Yet, somehow a person always surfaced who was taken by the little pup's charms and soon it was a done deal.

This yearly trek to Kenya began 15 years ago, each year bringing with it a plethora of cultural surprises, opportunities, joys, grief and just plain disappointment–not necessarily in that order.

Because of mzungu's (aka white person) trusting nature and habitual inability to plan ahead, she landed in some fairly precarious situations. Yet over a spanse of that time this mzungu learned to navigate these recurring challenges and merely chalk it all up to, well, unreliable living. The brittle, yellowing pages of her journals were merely a repository of her life in Kenya; that remarkable adventure-filled country where she:

- Learned to eat chapati, Ugale, rice and beans as a daily staple.
- Lived among Kenyan families
- Washed her clothes in Lake Victoria

- Learned a modicum of Swahili
- Learned to love Tusker and Pilsner beers
- Fought to keep the title deed to her plot of land
- Appeared in the High Court to combat corruption
- Swam in the waters of Lake Victoria oblivious of the hippos underneath her
- Rescued a half dozen street boys, giving them a modest home on her land.
- Marveled as the street boys planted mboga and maize on that land
- Riding on the back of a motorbike, carried a day old infant to the nearest clinic
- Came to know people from the Luo, Kisii, Kikuyu, Maasai, Acamba and Luhya tribes
- Had a small sailboat built; painted it herself
- Capsized the boat into Lake Victoria -described in" The Birth of the Yahweh"
- Joined with local families to begin a school for orphans living in parks.
- Rode endless miles in matatus (buses) on piki -pikis, and in tuk-tuks
- Loved and treasured African wildlife on the Maasai Mara, at Tsavo, and at Mt. Kenya
- Became at home on the streets of Nairobi, Mombasa, Kakamega, and Nakuru
- Shared the warm Indian Ocean waters with camels cooling off in the shallows
- Invested in a dozen start-up biasharas (businesses)
- Bought two Piki-Pikis, (motorbikes) & one boat motor for needy friends
- Watched corrupt politicians spin stories for control of the government
- Cried as she saw Kenya falling into destructive chaos during the 2007 post-election violence
- Took a side trip to Madagascar
- Returned home, weary every time from the 22 hour flights over seas and countries that became as familiar as her back yard.

Despite the many mistakes that Mzungu made due to her ignorance of Kenyan culture and tradition, she was always pulled back there year after year. Her Kenyan life became a work in progress, a spiritual evolution, an addiction that she couldn't shake.

On her return each time, her American friends would ask "Where are you?" while the Kenyans would say "You're back!"

To the recurring question of "What do you do over there? What church are you with?"

The answer always remained the same
"No church, no organization, just me"

"So, Quince, do you think she really did all that stuff?"

"No question, Dakota. Our human couldn't make all that up."

The journals still remain shelved in chronological order waiting to be revisited and hopefully brought back to life for others to read in disbelief.
"Hmmmm "she often ponders, "those stories would work well for my UNRELIABLE LIVING book. I need to get to that someday"

JUST BETWEEN US

As can be expected, our animals have their own lives apart from their humans.
　It is rare to access these erstwhile antics inasmuch that there is no verbal communication between us and them. Though this point can be challenged by some humans.
　Because we now find ourselves in that magical netherland where nothing is impossible, it behooves the reader to ease-drop into some of the most interesting of our creature spirits.

　Parakeet Murphy: "Well, you know, Snoopy, that little incident grounded me until I could regrow my tail feathers!"

　On an otherwise normal day in their California home, Murphy was enjoying a free-fly out of his cage. Hound Snoopy, who had never been a proper hunter, suddenly took it upon himself to make a hapless lunge in Murphy's direction. The next thing their human knew, Snoopy was carrying his little prey up the stairs, screeching and flapping its wings in protest. Running after the canine . his human walloped Snoopy until he loosened his grasp on Murphy giving her a chance for escape. Feathers in the dog's mouth were telltale signs of the attack.

　"That really gave me quite a rush, Murph ! Hee, hee you looked more like a chicken, then a bird after that, haha"
　"Your jollies at my expense, Snoop. You never did learn to hunt " chirped the still disgruntled parakeet.

　Adding to the conversation, Cockapoo Noche reminds her horse friend of a similar harrowing time between them.

　"Well Babe, I guess that by now you've sorted out how you put an end to my earthly life. It was your clumsiness in getting loaded into that trailer that put me into this new existence."

Babe: "Aw-w-w-w Noch…I am sorry about that. I never could get the hang of being loaded into a truck. Horses are supposed to PULL carts and wagons, NOT be hauled around in them!"

"Yeah right ! On one of your tries you stepped smack in the middle of my little old body!"

"It's not like I have a rear view mirror, pal; I was spooked by all that nipping at my heels!"

Those few minutes put a stop to the whole idea of transporting Babe to the new house.
Noche was scooped up by her human and rushed to the nearest Vet, where upon hearing the news that the little creature could not be saved, the human asked for time alone as she caressed Noche on the cold examining table.

"Thank you my precious Noche for being with me all these years. I know it was hard on you, but you stuck with me through thick and thin. That new baby that wanted to take your place in my heart, the crazy life with that large family, and all the moves I put you through. Thank you my Noche. Thank you so much. I love you"

The vet came in with the syringe.

"Oooo, this feels so-o-o- warm and good" the pup was saying, but those words couldn't reach her human. The sobbing was too loud.

ABOVE AND BEYOND-OUR STORIES

Since the idea of Above and Beyond was still a mystery to earthling pups Dakota and Quincy, they asked for help in understanding it.

"Where exactly did you just come from?" Quincy queried.
"Yeah-and how did you get there in the first place?" says Dakota.

"Reasonable questions," thought Chloe, "coming from ordinary pups leading their ordinary lives."

Boss Cat Chloe, as usual, launches the discussion.
"Well, Dakota and Quincy, we can see how you'd be concerned, seeing us float around here, no longer needing kibbles or hay or kitty litter.

"Fact is that all of us creatures and humans came with a built in spirit when we hit the ground, so to speak. That spirit in each of us guided and propelled our earthly bodies through Life wherever Life took us. Then we realized we couldn't be on earth forever (no one ever is), and we had to be prepared for what was next. And the next step is the Above and Beyond, you see?"

"But exactly where IS this Above and Beyond?" asks curious Dakota." and can I come and visit?"

"Not quite my dear. You see, the Beyond is a place that goes on forever made up of spirits who have lived in gazillions of creatures through the ages. In that forever place we are Above all of the pain, heartache, wars, famine, and killing that's here on terra ferma. It may not be that bad for you, Dakota, but for some creatures it's what some folk would call …pure hell"

Quincy offers," yeah but it's not that bad everywhere, Chloe. There's a lot of comfort and love and good stuff happening too."

"So true, Quincy. I am just telling you what Above and Beyond means. The point is that none of us creatures can stay on earth forever, and how we take that step into the Beyond is important. Many humans talk about this step as death, or dying, passing away, or being deceased. The fact is, when it is time for any of us to leave our bodies, it's that step that puts us into that bright, beautiful, soft, happy, endless space, the Above and Beyond . Strange that so many humans are afraid of it."

"So-o-o-, Chloe. If that place is so great, what are all of you guys doing here?" asks Quincy.

We 're here because spirits have a choice about which creatures still on earth that they would like to help. We, being our human's furry family, decided to come on a check-up visit to see if our human is all right. After all, some of us spent our entire lives with her.
If our human runs into trouble we want to help, and that's where you and Dakota come in. We will teach you how to help if she needs it, and how to listen to our whispers and nudges."
"We're up for any help we can get, right Dakota?"
"Sure nuff , but don't the humans have Human spirits that come to help them?"

"Of course they do, but these days so many folks are so linked to electronic devices and want speedy answers to everything that when their Spirits might come calling they are too busy, or stressed, or just plain tired to feel them. Sadly they miss out on a lot of good spirit guidance."
"Quincy, you told me how our human dug a hole and buried that phone thingy"
Yes, she did, when she realized it was taking up too much of her life and probably blocking spirits around her; in it went, and she was free !"

After this briefing, Chloe lined up her creature spirits for their next task, that of telling Quincy and Dakota how they crossed over into the Beyond.

"MUFFIN !! You're first up."

"I was happily playing with the neighbors pups when I chased a ball into the road and WHAM ! One of those cars whacked me! And I was still young and pretty too! My human had to come and gather me up and start digging a place for my left-overs. It's a shame that she couldn't have felt all that peace that I did when I took that step"

"That's true" NOCHE adds. "When Babe stepped on my gut that day it sure hurt for awhile, but the doc helped me take that step because that body was NOT going to work for me after that!

Another resting place was dug next to Muffins, tears streaming down the face of the heart- broken human once again.

Kitty SoSo says "you and I were both really up there in earth years, Noche. We went down a whole lot of roads together. I took my step up there on the dry irrigation ditch. When the water began to flow it lifted me up and floated me down to the house. Topside, my fur was all perfectly dry and beautiful. My human was pretty surprised to find me that way, just peacefully floating to her.

NEW JERSEY MINK remembers, "My human's boyfriend took me to his place while she was away on a job at the Jersey shore. We often went to visit her there and how she did miss me!

One day the boyfriend showed up with tears in his eyes to tell my human that I'd been hit by a car and had taken my step beyond in quick fashion. This was just one too many losses for my young human

OREGON SNOOPY says," You always were one for drama, SoSo !

My step was a little rockier. My human began bringing me to work with her because the doc said that my lungs were giving out, and she didn't want to leave me home alone. So I'd sleep all comfy in the car during her shift and she'd check on me. But this one night as I got into the Honda, a seizure grabbed me and she knew that this was it. So she just held me close and talked softly until I slipped away. There we were, close and warm against each other until at last she had to let me go. She laid me down with a kiss.

CALIFORNIA SNOOPY knows about that, "Yeah those humans have a real problem with letting go of us. I went through that too. Even down to my seizure problem. She was in the laundromat there off Base, leaving me in the car, when I got it in my head to go find her.
So I hopped out the window, and wouldn't you know? I had one of my seizures right there before God and the world, but this one took me into the Beyond. She had to carry both me and the laundry back to the house, sobbing all the way"

From being a precious pup in Baltimore and Johns Hopkins to a California Air Force Base, Snoopy was always a jumping, happy presence when her human walked in the door. They were companions on camping trips to Big Bear, Lake Arrowhead, Death Valley and the California coast. Most memorable, Snoopy had her litter of pups on the human's bed as she slept. Second most memorable, Snoopy was the first to hear that her person had to turn around and work a 24 hour shift after only 6 hours of sleep, leaving her pup alone once again.

It seemed that former President Eisenhower needed nurses for a few days out at their home out in Palm Desert. Not a hard assignment, but…why her??
(8X10 black nd white of human and Snoop with her litter.

"What do you pack when you go to stay with the Eisenhowers?" she asked, looking into her Beagle's loving, liquid brown eyes.

"Dunno… but you better leave plenty of chow and get someone to check in on me !"

BABE remembers her Step over.
"I spent my last horse years at a neat place called Rock Springs Ranch where folks would come up from the Willamette Valley and pretend to be dudes for a week-end. The young cowpokes asked for me a lot because I was so good with kids. My wrangler, Sven, kept my human up to date on how I was doing. When the girls went off to college my human knew I would be happier hanging out with a herd of my own kind. She was so right"
"Strangely enough my human was writing a little book about me to send to the ranch when Sven told her I had just taken my Step. I had a lot of earth years for a horse, so when my body gave out Sven took

the best care of me, and told my human how great I was and then how missed by the little cowpokes. But now they had that little book all about my life that they could read when they came to the ranch.

The book cover of the story the human wrote about Babe's life – in Babe's own words.

"I had two good earth lives: one with my human family and one with my horse buddies"

With that the session ended.

Dakota mulls it over. "Geesh, what good stories. What good earth lives"
"Yeah" says Quincy. "I hope ours goes that good !"

So I'll let the group tell you in their own words, how it was for them to take that Step."

LIFE CHANGES THINGS

As life progresses, for many humans families may wane or disperse.
When this happens the furry creatures come in closer while family and friends often go farther away, geographically, emotionally, or otherwise.

Quincy says," My human has been in this pretty house for eight years now and still not one of her family has come to see her. It's not all that far and gosh knows she has made the trip to their place many times. I know it makes her sad, but Dakota and I try to make her think of other things"

"Yeah-like food and treats for us!" adds Dakota pawing her tasty chew.

Life takes children into their own families and professions. Life also takes beloved spouses into the Above and Beyond. Filling in the void are the dogs, cats, horses, goats, tropical birds, and even bunnies that happen to wander into the lives of the infirmed and aging humans. Now, with the pets of their advanced years, it becomes a matter of who will take that step Beyond first?
If the human goes first he/she leaves the companion pet at the mercy of strangers.
If the pet crosses over first, the human is left with an unfillable void in life.
He /she is not about to start looking for a new companion because none could take the place of the creature who just took that step beyond.

"That's where we spirits help out" says Chloe. "Through dreams and casual little visitations in the daily lives of their humans, we often bring comfort to them from this other side."

One lady who felt that her time was soon to come, left a note in her home that should she pass away, her cat, Smurf, should be "put to sleep" shortly after. That proved to be unnecessary since when the authorities arrived a day later to find Smurf, they found her in peaceful repose. She had already taken care of that herself as many animals are known to do.

Another fine old gentleman knew that his end was near and requested that the ashes of his beloved but very aged canine be joined with his; that they would be cast to the winds of the Catskill Mountains together. That was easily doone.

Pet stories are full of such events, all of which confirm the strong bond formed between humans and the creatures that rescued them.

Considering how to handle the last days of life remains a challenge for many. It's a strange mix of fear, sadness, dread, and yes, sometimes even happy anticipation. It is not hard to believe that pets and their humans assist each other through this mysterious maze when either -or both- have to take that first step Beyond.

The Spirits now consider how their roles have changed in the rescue of their human as the years went on, often without anyone knowing it except for notable holidays and rites of passage.

The discussion begins.

"As I see it," contemplates SoSo "Humans need us more at sometimes in their lives and less in others"

"That's right" agrees Muffin, "when those families are young and going in every direction They hardly know we're around. But their kids just had to have a pet "to learn to be responsible."

Babe recounts how often
she comforted her human

"Good luck with that. Who has time to walk us? To change our kitty box? To muck out the stall? It usually falls to Dad or Mom."

"Yeah, right" adds Sport. "Then the kids go off to higher education and we're left consoling the "empty-nesters But by that time the older folks have learned to love us."

"True enough, Sport, but they're free now and have a hankerin' to travel and there we are Farmed Out Again !!!"

On a more serious note, Babe remembers:

"My human came down to the barn once, kissed my soft nose as I nuzzled her handful of oats. Then I saw tears streaming down her face and felt her heavy heart. For not the first time, she wrapped her arms up around my neck, held tight and sobbed. Did the kid go off to college? Did a good friend take that step over? Did my human lose her job? It made no difference to me as long as she knew where to find me."

GONE MISSING

There are those in this furry family that, for various reasons, just went missing, as pets so often do. When pets leave like this it can be almost as heartbreaking as when they go Beyond, because they leave without explanation. But then, of course, some DO JUST COME BA CK !!! Those that did return are ready to spin their yarn.

"Spinning yarn? That's a real good start up for us cats, eh?"

"Yes, Zoe and I are a few of those who went missing more times than you can shake a stick at" says CHLOE.
"Once in a Mexican motel, my human checked out of our motel and couldn't find me anywhere. I was out cruising the neighborhood. Sniffing and peeing. My human had to leave but kept calling the office, leaving her number in case I surfaced. Finally, new people checked into our room and I eventually came back there for my meal. The new folks were surprised to see me and figured I must have a human somewhere. She was one happy "josenita" when she came to retrieve me."

BUDDY says he can top that.

"We were driving cross country to New York when we stopped in a neat little country inn"
I really needed to stretch my legs after a long day's ride, so while my human unpacked the car I took off to follow all those new country smells. One scent led to another til I went far afield. Turned out she was so beat from the drive that she never missed me. What a night I had out there! At first light I came back to our place and yipped. When that door was opened I saw one surprised and very happy human. Me too. I needed food"

CHLOE wants to top that.

"We were in our favorite Motel 6 in Imperial Beach, CA; it came time to leave and I disappeared. Again.
(I must have this thing about not wanting to get back into the car)
"Well, my human gave up, figuring the time had come for us to part ways, and drove off.
100 miles later, she got home and heard a message that I had resurfaced to the very room where we had stayed.
She turned the car around and headed west to get me.
"What's 300 miles between friends?"

NOCHE shakes her head as a distant memory creeps in.
"Well, I wasn't missing for that far, but it was for a long, long time.

Good Grief! it's that little pup!

I hopped into the station wagon along with a slew of kids when my human went into town on one of her trips for groceries and the usual kid-drop-off-for sports. In and out. In and out. In and out. So many drop offs that no one noticed til they got home that I was missing. My human drove the 10 miles back to town and asked around about me. Gas station? No. Parking lot? No. School? No.

It was with a heavy heart that she returned home without me. The tribe of kids were too busy to notice. Time passed, and I'm not a good judge of days and times, but I heard tell later that I was gone for over a week. It was up to me to trace the road back; across the busy highway, up that steep hill, then down the rocky road to our place. And I'm just a little tyke !!'

Noche had that right, She was a pretty small and delicate pup to be gone for over a week. It would remain a mystery to her human how she ever found her way home and who, if anyone, fed her in the meantime.

"I'll never tell!! "says Noche "But it sure was fun to get to the garage door at six in the morning and bark til someone let me in"

"I remember that day" BABE pitches in. "We saw you trotting down the road and tossed you a welcome. Then our human came stumbling out in her nightgown, cried like crazy and scooped you up"

"Yeah. I bet none of those kids would get a welcome like that."

"No chance, Noche. No chance"

These missing creatures are those who found their way back and happened to have a human who would do just about anything to find them. But sometimes the pets are taken out of a person's hands by some twist of events, making it impossible for them to return to their human.

Such was the case with BUDDY.

`After riding west coast to east, and back again, Buddy and his human stopped by a friend's house to spend the night. Walking around the golf course area the next day, Buddy was in his usual "off leash mode" as the women talked. After far too long, he never returned. They called, called and called. Being the really handsome dude that he was, perhaps he attracted the attention of a resident who proceeded to take him in. His dog license had a phone number no longer valid, so all efforts to contact his human had failed..

At long last, his human checked the county animal shelter. YES they did have him. NO they couldn't locate her. YES, a family came in and fell in love with the little guy, and off he went.

His human showed up only a day after Buddy was adopted out. She pleaded with the officer to let her have him back; if not, could she please tell the new family important things about him?

NO. NO.NO

They would never see each other again. (or did Buddy just tire of all of that travel and welcomed a change of family?)

LIFE IN THE HERE AND NOW

Chloe checks in once again about the state of affairs between Dakota and Quincy and their human.

"So, she must be older now from when I was there. What has changed Quincy?"
"Well, not very much. Cloz. At least not for me and Dakota. But it's another story for the world around us. People were locked into their places for almost two years because of a really bad spreading bug. Over a million people in this country died. It didn't get us"

"And that was a good thing" pipes in Dakota. "But then more bad stuff came down the pike. Terrible wars over there in Eastern Europe; and if that wasn't bad enough, people are getting killed right and left here in our own country. Getting shot dead in schools and grocery stores."

"You've got to be kidding !!!!" Chloe is alarmed
"No, she's right, Cloz. It's NOT a happy time here in the good 'ol U.S. of A."

And so it is, sadly the truth. The now older human has trouble even watching the NEWs because of all the heartache and division there is. Rather, she occupies herself with the new finch nests being built and the baby birds eventually taking flight. She loves the quail and bunnies who scurry under the fence, -and of course the occasional Bull snake.
Folks have still to emerge fully from the Covid lock-down, and prices are so high that her usual get-away trips are a moot point.
The daughter and grandkids are so far away that there's no coming to Gramma's house for cookies; no going to piano recitals or soccer games.

"No family visits ain't all bad, She's not keen on house cleaning and really hates to cook!"

NOCHE adds "Yeah that tribe that she was married to found that out in a hurry ! Who wants to sit ten people down to a meal for three squares a day?"

More than once their human had pondered how really nice it would be to be less vital to the comfort, security and happiness of others. Now at last she knew; and it was feeling pretty good.

The daily lives of the human and her two canines bordered on absolute contentment.
Meal prep was now merely opening a can of dog food or taking a handful of the dry variety and sliding it into their dishes.
Daily exercise consisted of the pups having free run of the nearby desert, pausing to snuffle and dig deep into a hole that promised to deliver some sort of critter. They always came up empty but enjoyed the hunt.
On the home front, there was always the occasional gracefully winding bull snake, a covey of quail or a darting jackrabbit to capture their attention. Both canines would merely sit and watch the wildlife pass by. That is until cousin Coyote trotted past, caring little about their frenetic barking.
Life was going on as usual until the pups heard a strange sound coming from their human's study.

"Dakota? Do you hear that? What's that noise?"

"I Dunno Quince. Let's go see"

The pups peek around the door jamb only to find their human tapping away on the keys of her Underwood typewriter.

"What IS that thing?"

"Dunno, but it seems to be putting words out on that piece of paper rolling out of it."

Indeed, their human was at last obeying her decades long impulse to write. She had dug deep into the recesses of her travel journals and gleaned what had most affected her the in those adventures.
"I can see it now, Quince. The words say something like unreliable living"

Their human kept pounding on the old keyboard, the memories spewing out in torrents.

RE-THINKING AFRICA

"So-o-o- Mom, don't you think you're getting a little old for this kind of thing?
I mean, you could've been killed over there already , never mind ending up in an African jail"
"Mmmmmm"
Coffee tepid.
Clink clink, the spoon on the cup.
(Yes, there was that, she thinks)

"And they keep stealing from you. Look at all the money you've given over there1"
Mmmmmmmmmm
Eyes closed, deep breath.
Slow exhale
(taking is in their blood. I just keep giving them transfusions)
"Why can't you just stay home, learn bridge, watch your grandkids grow?"
Mmmmm
(Nice, but a little boring)

A chair drags impatiently away from the table, dishes clatter into the sink, footsteps pound away.

A last sip of tepid coffee.
mmmmmmmmmm
(If I give up Africa, I'd have to give up unreliable living)

THE SPIRITS DECAMP

After their prolonged visit to their earthling counterparts, the spirits from Above and Beyond were ready to return home.
As was Boss Cat Chloe.

"Well, I think it's all pretty well firmed up here . Quincy and Dakota have a good handle on how to help our human. They're a good pair."

"Yeah" agrees Sport. "Good thing you found Dakota when you did"

"I like the way our human guards all the springtime bird nests around their place and even counts how many babies fly off each year." adds parakeet Murphy.

"Those visits from her family that never happen might still be a problem"

"Only if our human makes it a problem. I think she has plenty to keep her busy"

Babe adds," It sure was swell all of us being together again. That was the best part !""

"Yep, we're the Furry Family on both sides of life. Someday those three will be right there in the Above and Beyond with us. Everyone comes eventually"

With that, Chloe called in Dakota and Quincy to tell them the plan.

"Well, guys, it's time for us to take off now, back to our Above and Beyond. We all think you're doing so good with our human that we're cutting you loose to finish up on your own"

SILENCE.

"Hey, you've got it down. The two of you know how to protect and care for our human"

SILENCE

"Really-you can do it !"

SILENCE

Dakota cries out "I wanna come too.. to that great Above and Beyond !"

"No dear," Chloe reassures," you can't come just yet. Your job is to stay here and be sure your human stays o.k. All three of you will join us, by and by"

"She's right, Sister" chimes in Quincy. "We have a good life here and I'd be darn lonely without you Dakota. So we'll stay."

That settled, the Furry and Feathery Family Spirits took a collective deep breath and as they slowly exhaled they were caught up into that soft, warm, loving jet stream that would take them back to Above and Beyond. Floating freely, dancing and singing they were almost home.

"CREATURES THAT HAVE SAVED ME"

"CREATURES THAT HAVE SAVED ME"

Printed by Libri Plureos GmbH in Hamburg, Germany